T0158390

A Night on the Lash

for Maggie

A Night on the Lash

Graham Mort

seren

Seren is the book imprint of
Poetry Wales Press Ltd
Nolton Street, Bridgend, Wales, CF31 3BN
www.seren-books.com

The right of Graham Mort to be identified as the
Author of this Work has been asserted in accordance with
the Copyright, Designs and Patents Act, 1988.

ISBN 1-85411-375-5

A CIP record for this title is available from the British Library.

The publisher acknowledges the financial assistance
of the Welsh Books Council.

Printed by Gwasg Dinefwr, Llandybie.

Cover photograph: Michael Hiscocks.

Back cover portrait: Richard Mort.

Contents

Cuba Libre at the Café España

Blueprint

Blue light is lifting footmarks from the snow, the way
fingerprints are filched from the scene of a crime.

The village gapes under its exclamation of pines,
its charred smudge snowing blackly onto snow.

No moon; first stars sniping through cold, a cat sniffing
at open doors, slinking from silence to silence.

The dead sprawl on settees, last gestures squandering
their hands, their blood a darkening memory of heat.

Lights waver on the road; the cat flees engines, the creak of
tyres, voices, cameras flaring at the houses' opened mouths.

Then ruffled hair, shucked clothing, the huddle in the ravine,
their papers blowing away, the mountain much as it was.

In the barracks there is slivovitz, sliced sausage, the scalded
throats of the militia, a naked bulb shuddering in song.

Dawn shows a line of women, their children's questions
hushed, their shoes' diaspora printed on a crust of snow.

They stoop under bundles, under the present tense of history.
This is a new year dawning; what begins here, begins again.

Eclipse

You're back tonight. Outside my door,
your face dark through its frost.

It's thirst that brings you; don't pretend
otherwise. Your lips are dry.

Tonight only the moon is quenchable.
We watch from the window's slit:

its fist salutes from the mountain's
epaulets of snow.

The moon bounds, the street brightens
under lost gravity.

Moon is pure meniscus, water's gleam
in a well's sleeve.

The night digs its own long shadow,
spades it into that hole.

Our duel is on again, you say. The moon's
tossed dollar turns on its

shot-out rim. Your mouth is hot. Now
blood marbles the moon

its mist spreading in fine droplets
sprayed from our kiss.

Stars' shrapnel cools, still white-hot,
still screaming outwards.

Before you slept I saw the orange
moon clear like lipstick

smeared from a mirror. Before you woke
a whole night later, I saw

a shadow tremble on your eye then fall,
splashing into moon.

Reportage

The river running with its scut of foam,
that August of rain.

Nights in the car under cover of trees,
watching the road liquidise.

Taking down the weather's shorthand,
its stammering Derry brogue.

Gardens overgrown, cold-frames smashed,
a lace of cabbage leaf.

That neighbour chancing it, a newspaper
folded over his head.

Then one day of sun, drying out the evidence
of summer's ruin.

Drizzle hushing the ash of barbecues
left to cool at dusk.

A line of policemen swishing into grass,
re-run on the nightly news.

A bullet-hole in a blue temple *Wouldn't
think to harm a fly.*

Then more rain, weather's clichés falling,
its column inches being filed.

My Father's First Day at Work

Half asleep in the grey smudge of September
rain a carthorse sneezes towards fleeting
dazzles of the sun.

Its hooves click on a cobbled yard, its hide
flinches from my hand and rain trails its silver
filaments from tilted hooves.

The horse dreams me from its sweat of sleep
or I dream the horse, the day itself,
that smell of soap and leather,

a fly entering its nostril, this mane tangling
my fingers, the way its neck is coarse, hot,
and kissable with rain.

If I try to look away from these lost days
a boy distracts me, enters the yard
to set down pails of milk

and smiles towards me through a looming war
and does not recognise me and hardly tastes
the bit of work between his teeth.

Birdwatching

Minesmere RSPB Reserve

This timber smells of creosote and church,
a kestrel's flick-book Christ is hung outside
and silent as the spiders wrapping flies
in every torture-chamber of this hide.

Water glitters where it's cut by sun,
a redshank flurries from the lake and sings,
a tern slices cliffs of superheated air,
on every stump a cormorant dries its wings.

Sizewell glimmers like an exposed brain,
two hi-tech swans plane in to land on skis;
we're hiding from the birds, not them from us
and sudden death is furtive in the trees.

Autumn teaches the young sycamores to die;
the resurrections sown are spring's poetic lie.

Desire

Think of it out there, glinting;
a chromium hinge in the swung door
of a saloon bar, the membrane
of a tiercel's eye sliding from a wet
branch in woods where suddenly
no birds sing and nothing moves.

Think of it stifled: a man holding
back his orgasm, a woman faking
her sighs, a fighter weighing-in each
gram of his body's precious meat,
the surgeon peering to unblock a
blood vessel thudding with life.

Think of it as something ending or
beginning, the rip of gas lighting a
coffin's sheen, a motorway pile-up
where cars slew windscreens, skid-marks
smoke, where no one knows why or
took notice of the warnings anyway.

That's how it goes, so think of it:
a spark in dry grass, the hillside
waving its blanket of smoke, a sick
man rising and falling into sickness
again; an open car, crossed hairs
focusing a stalker's eerie calm.

Think of it arriving unnoticed,
except by virtue of its stealth.
Think of it as grief or as rejoicing;
virginity lost then remembered;
a credit card which bought you
everything spent into the red.

Think of it as aftertaste, your skin
perfumed by other skin, bones
and smeared glasses left at table.
Think of it fading the way we fade,
our rage to go on flaring into futures
that mirage over drifted sand.

Think of it out there, tangible
beyond these metaphors.
Think how nothing dies but this
thing fills the void, how nothing
ever lasts or should. Think of it:
then watch your back and wait.

Distance

Gridlocked, the station broils in lassitude;
rails glint in angle-grinding sun, girls saunter
in short skirts, a porter shunts trolleys, a cat
woos pigeons with disingenuous charm.

An unshaven man, a woman in a yellow dress taste
a kiss, tentative as asking in a foreign tongue;
no train comes, but heat crumples hills beyond the
town hall roof, its copper cupola and lying face.

No train. The town is held at two o'clock, no ransom
for its golden hands, but girls still pass, so something
must be happening somewhere close. The cat cocks
its ears and stares, the porter wipes his face, the woman

sighs, the man rubs stubble, fumbles for a match.
Headlines wilt on the news stand, calamities
settle into columns, calmed until we read them,
feel something – nothing maybe – treading

two o'clock like water deeper than our legs.
You're screwing your heel into pink chewing
gum, sighing in your yellow frock. Elsewhere,
the train shimmers in its chemise of heat,

I smoke this cigarette, watch your breasts pant
under their glaze of salt. I'm through with kissing you,
I think, but can't say exactly why or what has snapped
loose from its attenuated moment. Pigeons parachute

from gutters, the town hall time is two, the train arrives.
I watch those girls watch a woman ask a man a question
which slakes his face the way dust takes rain. Your eyes
brim with slamming doors and you're asking me again,

What's wrong? What's wrong?
All this, I say, taking your arm, taking the pulse
of your body's closeness to mine, its distance
from the sun. *All this.*

Walking Home on New Year's Day

Two a.m. First-footing a whitened road,
hills gleaming with ice, hoar-frost
curdled on each wall and iron gate.

Earth skates under Orion's belt,
the road sways, the moon sinks,
licked away by ebbing dark.

Sheep cough in fields of tarnished light,
snow just holding back its mass
of purest sleep, the uncertain edge

of wakefulness we're walking now.
I tell you something strange and wonderful
to pass the time: how water frozen

under zero's brink can still stay fluid
against all odds, how its molecules
cheat Nature's laws, brimming

at the very frontier of solidity, like old
men slugging strokes against the
deepening current of their lives.

Supercool superfluity of motion: a miracle!
Until one snowflake falls to slush whole
lakes into the stillest blues of instant ice.

It's said our Universe could hold its own
dark matter in such breath-held states, that
any particle colliding there could in a blink

unpick the cross-stitch of the stars.
We pause to think about those aeons of ice,
mull a slow kiss spiced with wine –

annunciation that we'll never change or die.
I pull away, walk on, look up to feel the first
snowflake landing on my eye.

Black Dog

The dog is watching your house, the black dog in
the grass of sorrows, down on four paws, staring
as thunderheads gather, watching for a gleam
of lights, some wild expectancy of curtains pulled

or song snatched or steps waltzed above dawn's
apricot abyss. The black dog points its ears,
snuffles a wind of scent-whorls, hears the radio, a
turning page, your heart in quiet rooms, a knife

against bread, a spoon clinking an empty cup; it
smells your sweat, hand-printed on the mail, and
something else, close to fear or nakedness. A new
day fills rooms with dread of mawkish tunes or her

hand slanted on an envelope. The dog lies doggo,
Mnemosyne clamped in its mouth, that willing bitch.
The turned page is blank; music drops like a vase,
ivy blows against the window, its inane metre

counting to nothing, night and day. The dog runs from
a dream of welted black, lopes through inky streams,
leaps a creosoted fence, an oil-skimmed ditch, gallops a
marsh of burning tar. Brought by a call above hearing's

pitch, the dog keeps vigil and when admitted to the
house, stinks of rain, wet hair, sour yeast and shit.
This sable hound shakes silver from its coat; you
feed it from a crazed blue bowl, stroke its narrow skull

where you exist in analogues of sound and scent.
The dog is dark as a full-stop or a clot of feeding flies;
it could be shot or gassed or pricked to sleep. That
thought's no use. The dog's eyes fill with amber light

that tents you on twin globes. You're in too deep,
door-stepped by the tenth and most reliable muse.

Later

I have you dressed in blue, Victoria plum,
a dark old bruise, a dress of fine-spun wool,
its patina of age.

I remember this, your hand held up,
plucking out some word, some jagged
stone you couldn't spit.

Your eyes are almost lost, shadowed in
a room which smells of orange peel,
almonds, the must of bundled suits
that you've brought home again.

Memory floods, spins to a small pool
in which you move towards me dressed
in indigo, hands veined around that fruit,
that hidden gist, perhaps the clenched
word you need to place in mine.

It's not that I remember all you couldn't
say or let go of, that's not it.

But when I touched your arm, mouthing
that useless thing – which fates are best
in the end – your heart's struck fish leapt
to knock away my hand.

Anderson Shelter

Each time that smell returned:
damp hessian, spider's breath,
creosote and black earth crumbling
from the garden fork.

Ribbed steel burned under his
palm; a blazing afternoon spilled
laburnum blossom outside
in the garden's glare.

Dust motes glittered, floating
as scattered spores of light;
the shelter was a dream ship
drifting from the land.

Now he's staring from a house
where someone like him used
to live, leaning on vinegar-
scented window glass

intent on what is left of
what it was that held him:
the ebb of afternoons
that might be happening still

if the boy had let them, not risen
to play pirates, dirty his knees,
blow dandelion clocks at the
yellow ensign of the sun.

Afterlife

It starts with a journey's end, arrival,
uneasy sleep; then the B&B's stripped
bed, a window opened to admit rank mist,
an early morning walk that will always
be too early for the town to light with life.

Empty holiday homes, a beach where
scuppered monkfish retch on shingle,
a line of tarred shacks, winter light glinting
on the price of fish, on enamel scales that
hold something absent in their balance.

Then a row of clinkered hulks, their flaking
names. Winches hauling fog. Couples arm in
arm, huddled against the future, never free
from habits of companionship, their eyes
wishing days could begin with things visible
or closer to their tongues.

Voices shout at dawn's smother, something
arriving beyond the ebb-tide's misted groynes,
its marshes and Martello tower, lank lagoons
and dry-docked yachts, beyond its glimmer
of resurrecting light where God's chapped
hands cup the tab-end of the sun.

This is journey's end again, coming near.
This is arrival. Listen: this is here.

Presence

Snow in all the windows. Two hundred miles
of steel. Delays. A burning head where
he's hammered too much gin.

Wheels thrum, water gleams in ditches,
winter's dregs spilling in a mind full of other
winters, other journeys, days.

A man at a canal yells to his alsatian bitch;
the backs of brick-built houses pass and people
somehow keep on living there.

Maybe if he watches he'll see a shutter pulled,
a killer's hands shadowed at the throat
of some impossibly lovely girl.

But the man opposite needs to talk, unhooks his
Walkman, bringing a tinnitus of slide guitar
played the way only Texans can:

so slow and so mean. The train enters a white-
out where fields should be green and English,
but snow's fever is forgetting them.

The ring-pull hisses. He pours tonic water's
quinine dose. Mosquitoes zing in a reed hut;
a Portuguese prospector dies in his delirium

of wealth, the river takes away rubber and
gold dust; the Indian is tattooed blue, the
dugout's prow turns water's bronze.

Rails syncopate. The man opposite describes
a Japanese border back home where he's planted
celandines, a rare foxglove. Back home.

The tonic water can rolls to the table's edge;
they gulp heated air, then brakes are
laid on hard, their balm of stasis.

A trainfull of people shudders and slows,
scattering their thoughts beyond a place's,
stark, enamelled name.

He's listening to the names of flowers,
imagining a garden, a woman he could
love walking by the pond's fringe of

irises, the centre of each eye wide with
longing. He notes the man's lank hair,
endures his low, legato voice.

There is something between them now,
something that only speech has built. He sips
gin's juniper sting, wonders what kind

of thing that is, how much more real than
the stairs to his room, the bed where a novel
still lies open for his mind to write in;

where sheets are scented with a presence that is
not flowers or woman, that fits him close as
sweat or a suit of darkest clothes.

Myson Midas

At first it worked like a clock, the timer's plastic
teeth gritted in the day's hours to vent that puff of
steam each dawn: a gun to raise the drowned.

Then radiators ticking, water climbing the house,
a wash of heat that dried the air, warped window-
frames and kept us from the snow. One day it

stalled, monarchical and crazed, boiling paint-blisters
until the gas-man calmed it, his hands soothing it
the way a shepherd lambs a softly bleating ewe.

It sulked for weeks. The gas-man almost lodged with
us: checked resistances, changed sensors, untangled
wiring looms, fingered pipes to track a fading pulse

Intermittent faults are hard to find. Too true. What he
couldn't guess, his hands groped for in gloom lit by
rubies on the diode board. He felt a drip and

staunched it, clipped strands of copper, coaxed
gaskets, Morsed free a sticking valve, and with a fine-
haired brush did archaeology on seams of dust.

Dog-days of random heat ensued; we never knew what
happened when we left the house, if scalding plumes or
flutters of the pilot flame erupted there to flare and cool.

One day I found him, head-pressed to the boiler's guts,
swearing in iambics at the bastard thing, his hands em-
bedded, coaxing hope. They came out carbon-stained

but cupped success: a ghost-flame lit his worn, angelic face.
He left for good; an absence; idling heat. Now, at two a.m.
a taxi tracks the street. Someone steps home alone to

bear their empty house. We lie awake, touch fingertips,
hear rooms exhale last whispers of the miracle his hands
have brailled here for our fumbling hands to read.

Moth At Llançá

All night circling, its antennae feathering
against blinds, wings ticking on white walls
where we lie in memories of our lives.

Then grasshoppers staving our pillows with
insomniac haste, as if we lay until dawn
in a sea's long fever of unrest.

The bread van mutters smoke, sounds its horn;
our shoulders touch, burned by a fallen sun.
Sheets lie in a heap, their cotton rumpled

like the mountain outside, still asleep.
Air sings. The moth on the sill, face-down,
folds death's head in its wings.

General Pinochet, Retired

He tidies the lawn, scuffs toadstools with
his heel, rakes them like a mare's flank,
then wanders from the sun.

Nights have gnawed the apple to a gourd;
it brings ants which scatter on the table
until his finger stops their run for it.

The same finger strops dew from a crow's
feather, which he arranges with the apple
into the stillest life.

He reads a newspaper, strokes the table's
planed narrative of seasons, regards
the pale shades of his infamy.

He listens to the maid in the kitchen, lets
his finger drift to the feather, pictures
wing-tips spiralling into light.

He's thirsty from his work, calls her to
bring him lemon juice, iced water beading
a glass. But she is busy some-

where behind him, salting almonds,
slicing limes, singing to no one
of Iquique's bone-dry winds.

Amniocentesis

Kerry hills' piled turves smouldering;
far off rain, thunderclouds, a mackerel
spine of light splitting over sand.

Packing a few things, flinching
from a bumble bee, sun on her
arms, the road a necessary
scar on the day.

Sea's pewter tongues licking
away the strand; then a skylark
falling silent, then a knife chopping
sage in the kitchen where her sister
is helping out.

Cut lemons, zest, haste;
the sea's swell a vast
optimistic lie, the windows
repeating her every move.

Her shoulder scalding with
impossible sun, the mountains
put there to tell her:
Live with this.

Fuchsia, montbretia, willowherb;
the sea murmuring, stammering
to pronounce itself at the edge
of things –
soon, now, the road
soon, now, the road –
this memory still happening
and will not stop.

Heirlooms

A pearl, she said, *draws all things
to itself.* And she held them knotted
in her fingers the way mushrooms
glow in the roots of trees at dusk.

I thought of a pearl's intimacies:
a diver's blood hurtling in his lung,
the song, tidal in a singer's throat,
that faint pulse basking at her hands.

A pearl which is an oyster's tumour –
the plank in its blurred eye – globes with
breath's mist of adoration or envy.
I wanted to say: *Don't die. Not yet.*

Those evenings at the Steinway her voice
trembled up minor scales, brimming with
a song's old, burnished hurt then resting
in the black velvet of her sleep.

Once she saw these broken in the street,
scattered to the gutter, a surprising hail
I gathered up then re-strung on her
clavicle's fine harp; none lost, not one.

Watching the sea that last time, she said:
The waves are loose pearls, jostling.
And I paused, wanting to say how the sea
is the mind's irritant, how memory is a

pearl held then let go of, falling and
turning less brightly. But I said
nothing, watching her neck turn back
to the waves' quiet exclamations.

The Presidential Sleep

Bell towers are tongueless, houses
crack and fall into the listless streets;
leaves whisper to themselves, windless
days store up abandoned heat.

Satellite dishes cup their ears, strain
towards the antic south; their wave-
lengths are scrambled consonants in
a lunatic's aphasic mouth.

A road runs over its own aftertaste:
creek-bottom salt, dried blood, bad luck.
Blizzards of crushed cement sift into
wind-screens on abandoned trucks.

Cats are wild for pigeons over sagging
roofs, dogs starve without a human hand;
dust-devils resurrect and whirl from
the suction of the land.

I'm guessing this, remembering my
dream of futures haunted by such fear,
the incubus of nothingness that cuckoos
out what's now and here.

I'm reaching towards unsplit rock,
clutching the crooked staff of speech;
quartz crystals shine, then dim, their
liquid moments trickling out of reach.

Demagnetised

You fumble a takeaway foil tray
onto the oil-dark chaos of his desk;
one Madras chicken, a garlic naan
his revved-up pancreas might risk.

His morning's spent on a mobile phone
copper-greasing metal deals; outside
the lads strip out each wreck from
glove compartments to the wheels.

The cabin's piled with wiper-blades,
acid-free batteries, radio-cassettes
that spew tape like you'll spill your guts
about this bastard's bag of tricks.

A Gilletted ear leaks rubies as he drops
his bucket mouth and bolts the lot,
then spanners out one rusty benediction:
This fucking bastard's fucking hot.

The crane glissands an Escort past –
God, pity his wife is all you think –
its crumpled bonnet's dumped, crushed,
then cubed into a neatened life.

The boss hoists his balls, belches,
scraps his tinsel plate and farts;
windscreen crystal snows like tears
freezing over broken hearts.

Later, you'll scrawl his name on his
unfunny, photocopied arse, pin it to
the bulletin board he rates so smart,
then update his logbook, getting in

each time and place he never rendered
unto the Revenue what was due;
anonymous, you stitch him up for each
time he had then disregarded you.

Sun's low-beam lights up camomile,
its petals drooping, Arctic White;
that Nova's willing mascot nods,
then crashes as the magnetism's cut.

Off to the post, you watch the lads renew
a resprayed ringer's everlasting life;
winching in an engine, welding seats,
erasing chassis numbers with a knife.

The clock glides back over motorways,
near-misses, still days, country lanes
and lay-by lovemaking it never registered:
that row of noughts makes everything begin again.

Feral

Footloose, it gathers impressions faithlessly,
defining things which remain undefined, not
seeking love nor expecting it, but expert
in similitude.

Describing breakers on a beach then riding them,
a tideline of frayed plastic, gulls' cries, then dusk
in which a human voice is broken
to the point of tears.

The next moment seducing out the scents of thyme
or tar or rotting fish, the touch of wet ferns or fresh-
tasting figs and every part of speech
brindling with appetite.

Slinking through sleeping towns, licking its paws,
napping in the undertaker's doorway, waking
for star-rise, stretching, noting the anguish
in a hurrying woman's heels.

Then the tricks of darkness across rooftops where
shadows lurch and breed; the assignation
of each thing with words and its turning
back to dumbness.

On the move again over damp lawns, under
hung sheets sagged by dew or frost, watching
a fox redden the golf course, rooks gathering
for early mass, a girl's stark body rolled

from a car into the future's chilled forensics.
Then padding across a bridge too frail to
take its weight, alert in each sense, intent
on everything and fiercely satisfied.

Leaping from roof to roof, moving over streets
and under them, escaping notice, arching its
back at its own scream shocked onto
a pane of blackened glass.

Would you trust it, take such a creature home?
To purr the days away, lie flat as the pages
in a book? Then out all night and fucking
so wild it sounds like death?

Lapping the moon from a saucer, licking its neck-fur,
hypocrisy's winding-gear grinding in its throat,
soliciting your hand, your love, your kitchen's
offal, heat, and blood.

Now ignoring you: hesitant, decisive, fey, its pupils
slashed in irises green as jealousy or jade,
its footsteps hardly rhyming
as it pads away.

Batsville

One night reading Raymond Chandler alone
in her apartment, she found a bat floating
face-down in the toilet bowl then called me,
the phone narking at my shell-like.

More Harpicide than homicide, she cracked,
adding that lacking a bat-slice she'd fished
it from the pan, dried it on a windowsill until
it twitched alive, each moment of resurrection
inching it from light.

But blind to love, ignoring her, shimmying side
ways, a dame in broken heels reverse-casing
the joint then clinging to the wall outside: a
sad suicide-stunter but no bored french-fry
munching crowd yelling *Jump, goddammit,*
jump!

It left in its own good time, its wings turning
their creased pages, the plot fumbled and
thickening, so that she wondered what it was
she'd just read and whether she'd understood
a single word, asking me *Will it be alright*
out there?

And me like a two-bit lawyer already working-
up its alibi from death, a cover-story to fool
her blind: unerring radar, navigational stunts,
a hunch of pure hope for that airborne prince
of darkness it was surely curtains for

this time.

Christmas Eve, 2000

It dawns, its innocence unfazed by fine snow
dusting city streets, discarded carrier bags,
McDonald's trash or Empire heroes multi-
coloured bulbs have climbed.

Sleep gutters to another day; the yellow stains
that strays leave melt buds already purple
tips of trees that ghost the park under its
shuttered cloud. They'll stay

those clouds, till dusk, and so will these ascetics
stifling yawns to spend the day in cardboard shrouds,
fearful of the neon-held-back dark, dossing
at entrances where nights

begin and have no end of questions cooling the mind's
vestigial heat. Fat Santa rides a sky of fairy lights,
Christmas Eve turns to Christmas Day,
wind turns easterly, snow to sleet

that melts away the false nativity of streets
and lays a black road there, each tarmacadam
tongue pronouncing a vacuous, benighted,
Where? The question rustles

in its void, the way a preacher's voice rakes
empty pews, the way a thinning congregation
shuffles feet with cold or trees drop leaves or
sleepers wake in ancient news.

Geese from a Timber House

That summer house. Its veranda and pitch-
pine frame, cracked windows, slant walls,
shot-up carpet straddling the stairs,
the smell of damp and pre-war family
holidays still seasoning each room.

Long days: reading, writing, watching the tide
trying to tear away the beach, rearing where
scores of geese steered south before the gales.
All over England rivers overflowed, the
railways had packed up and you were

travelling towards me, stranded on a train
with no real notion where I was. A borrowed
beach-house, that's all. The cuffs of my jumper
catching at a page, a coffee pot branding the table
like the thought of you, that we'd be together

and everything alright again, despite
those gales, the flypast of geese foretelling
worse to come. I wandered by each window,
hearing tiny shrieks of wind, watching
bushes tear their hair, and felt alive

with loneliness, wanting to mark a vee of
kisses in that favourite place behind your knee.
Then you rang and I was gunning the car
through floods to meet you at Saxmundham –
that fly-speck dotted on the map.

Night dropped. Tracks glittered into rain.
The train came late. Each mile of B road to
the coast was fraught with wind, high water,
fallen trees; then village lights shrank the dark
and I was opening our door into a stale

summer-scented past. We slept in its memory,
woke to calmer seas, to geese planing waves,
landrovers braked in the road, serious men
gathered in Wellingtons and woollen hats,
their fingers stroking walnut stocks.

We sidled through them for our walk,
trudged two miles through spray and shingle,
deafened by the sea. It was later, hunched over
whisky macs, the gas-fire drying our shoes,
we heard the guns begin to talk.

A Hole for Belgrade

First a dimple, then a crater, then tarmac cancer gnawing
its way from light like something the council or God
laid on without the usual paperwork.

Then a man with halitosis and a measuring wheel,
the sound of running water that might always
have been there. *You can never tell.*

That surprises him more than missiles hitting Belgrade,
mass graves turned over, an iron plough in his hands
as he dreams the news each night.

This year he shrugs off May blossom, ignores rhubarb,
beheads daffodils with scarcely a word to his neighbour –
the baker with a Polish past.

No one takes the hole away, which after all is only half
a hole; and who knows when a hole has stopped
growing, or just when half a life has passed?

Lying beside his wife at night who smells of hair dye, hot
nylon, unreachable loneliness, he sees the hole
as a suddenly emptied mouth.

Almighty Father. He skims in beautiful words, remembered
prayers, one childhood song in which *The big ship sails through
the ally, ally-o, the*

hole caves in, surprising him again – its lack of warning.
How can it do that? he asks his wife,
First nothing, then a hole?

She's wiping marmalade from her moustache, thinking
how she'd sliced oranges in a hot kitchen last
autumn, seduced the baker she hadn't known

was Catholic, until he came gasping Hail Mary's full
of grace. That night her husband lies puzzling over
the thought of taking lives to save them.

Then the sound of lorries, the council digger, hard-core
being tipped, arc lights, voices and a spade
scraping at his nerves.

But council men at night? *At night?* They leave the hole half-
filled, a plastic fence in place, chalk marks on the road –
the kind that spare the first-born.

Five daily papers later, nothing's changed, except more
rubble in Belgrade, more pictures of the dead unburying
themselves with newsprint blackened hands.

He watches the hole, there in the road, unhealed.
You'll stay, he says, *For ever and ever. You'll stay.*
Amen.

Streetlamp Lizard, Deià

Each day, delirious with dusk,
I freeze into my deadly station,
crawl from the sun's split husk
to flex my tongue's dumb ululation.

My four feet sucker to the lamp
that lets aloof a faint green light;
my eyes, unblinking, press death's stamp
on moths that flicker from the night.

Unmoved by stars above the town
that's lit by traffic, human speech,
I prey until dawn draws me down
from where I cling, cold as a leech.

Then gods that spare me for this work
haunt azure skies as huge-eyed hawks.

Washdays

A washtub, a washboard, a hot yard,
the man's anger chipping at bricks,
drawing his bride through her mangle
in the washday sun.

A lead pipe spurting at a grid where
slugs copulate in grease; the mill
chimney writing something high up
in smoke they can't yet read.

The man searching for work, the
wound under his demob suit itching,
its metal splinters burrowing towards
his lung. Then words blurting, then

the man's hand across the woman's
face, unexpected, like her tears;
everything here unexpected, except
poverty the end of war prophesied.

Womb-blood on a towel, the woman
washing it away with green soap eked
from ration coupons; only blood and
her husband's voice unrationed now.

A window gawping from the house,
the man's mother staring out, gauging
whiteness, an insufficiency of sweat
sudding the washboard. Each Tuesday,

the woman dabbing Dolly Blue on the man's
collars; then a child in her belly, sloshing as
she sways to the wash, away from the man's
voice, his speech fracturing, incomplete –

like the night never quite closing over her,
sleepless on pillows stuffed with down,
her head on a flock of birds snatched

from their fidelities in a far-off sea of ice.
The man hoisting the wet basket,
too heavy for her condition, their
sheets bleaching them out from the day,
their voices disappearing into sun,

vanishing from the room where his
mother hoards shillings in an Oxo tin,
spiders at another inquisition about her belly,
shopping bills, the Co-op divvy.

The wife stoops, takes a clutch of lupins
to his mother's sneered surety she'll
fill the house with bad luck or bastards;
instead she brings colours, warping light.

The old woman sulks by the wireless,
dwelling on free teeth, a pension, her own
husband sucked down into Ypres mud,
still young in his unmarked grave.

The woman remembers her own dead
mother dusting at a worn settee,
worshipping the front step, a donkey
stone yellowing decencies underfoot.

The man talks, his voice harping on lino,
distemper, a stairs-runner; the woman
arranging lupins in a scraped out jar,
the man's voice a rolling boil, his fingers

daily shaming her face. The woman,
imagines the child, not crying for it yet
because there is everything to cry for,
because tears are commonplace, like

ashes cast out each morning to the
dirt back where the child will play.
Once she helped a soldier die, his last
words nothing she could understand;

just another nurse, but her own soldier
lived, watched her from his bed as they
gathered around him, cooled his wound-
fever with starched white wings.

Now that wound twists his mouth, stitching
it with crooked speech. He never tried
to kill, he says, pointing the rifle anywhere,
letting it kick above his heart where

only hymns had kicked before. Then he
lay in rubble, hit; no pain, but fire blackening
him the way a belt buckle tarnishes,
the way a wound grows gangrenous.

She'd seen that too: a homesick, southern
G.I. boy smiling through a stench they couldn't
bear until he slipped away through choked
French verbs to the bayou's cloying dark.

These memories: the woman sitting with her face
in lupins; the man idling; the mother of the man
afraid in her own changed house; their washing
towing the garden into brightening wind.

Sun is machined into its lathe-cut arc;
the window cooling the woman's temple,
sky ravelling out an unspun hank of smoke
to swaddle the hootered town.

Days, seasons, nights. The earth dizzy,
the moon untrodden, acid from factory
chimneys rotting bricks and slate, the town
dying and growing, bringing the city's

overspill to new estates where they'll covet
a council semi, freeze his mother with a box
Brownie then bury her in the Baptist church,
her mouth pursed tight as cash.

It goes on: days wrapping them in rain, in sun, in breath. The boy-child at ease under her heart, his blood kicking at the cord, his clenched fists already sure of everything.

Radiotherapy

At the window where the days come in
and some escape, though the glazing's tight,
a woman stands, amazed, watching
something glow inside her like a pilot light.

The day is fading from the street where
wet leaves stick like pages of a book
left out and she is trying to read
the skin beneath their mottled look.

Things are everywhere: those trees,
those cars jostling at the roundabout,
the radio switched off, the t.v. blank, the sofa
worn at the arms where they sat

or made love on evenings when the music
or the food or wine was good; now she
has something to get on with, this glimmer
on her skin, this singing in her blood.

The something she'll excise, feel sorry for,
excusing her lopsidedness or lingerie
and laughing at the thing friends dread.
They demand solemnity, prefer curtains

drawn like sutured skin. Now when
they phone to get her through the night
she opens blinds to let the streetlamps in,
stands naked at the glass in hymns of light.

The Alchemist Next Door

What he does, you wonder, hearing
him clatter quietly to his wheelie bin
on dark mornings, fumbling with black bags
when the sky is pure frozen sleep.

All night his house lights burn and you
picture him at a table etching crystals
from dull stone, their brilliance ringing
his eyes with amethyst.

Or when the bags squelch see him
butchering body parts, hands bloody,
his bedroom an abattoir, his fridge a
skull-house, backlit and grinning.

On cold days his starter-motor rasps
abraded splines, starts at the third try
when he drives off to some kind of work,
wiping the windscreen with a rag.

Or never works, but parks to watch
the windows of a certain house where
a woman drowns her face in silvered glass
and hums the cadence in his head.

You couldn't draw his face from memory
yet at weekends greet him, amiably
scooping the sundae of a frozen rose bed,
astonished by the paleness of his hands.

He watches you watching him alone,
the way your eyes absent themselves,
searching his soil for sharp serifs,
its sanskrit of fallen petals or of bone.

A Night on the Lash

The river's neon blusher is rising through rain,
through sewers and gutters and cast-iron grids,

through faked alibis, failed marriages, through
suicide and homicide and fumbled, sad affairs.

She's out alone tonight, lounging on a high stool,
wanting something more than this,

eye-lashes lowered, cheekbones cool against
a chromium rail. A single rum, her fingers

slack on the glass, her stacked heels rising
and falling with that song. Those lads

laughing in the back room, spinning pool
queues, strutting to the jukebox, born to

the manner, the lash, to everlasting pints
of Stella, baseball caps, unlaced trainers,

jeans loose against designer groins.
The lash cracks rain on glass, the river

glitters up slimed brickwork, plucking at
each streetlight's yellow blossom.

Blatant lips, an emptied glass, ice melting
the bar stool's itch against her thighs; her short

dress, parted breasts, the lads laughing at nothing,
but something pressing with its insistence to be

somewhere and someone. The lash coiling, her
tongue dipping, the last drop, the jukebox

telling us to dance or die, her fingernails
smoothing hair under the lights' hot knife.

Then the lads standing in a line, still laughing,
lashing the porcelain, asking dumbly

Is this what it means, to dance or die?
If only they could speak, lad to lad, but can't,

returning for another round to find that lass,
that slapper gagging for it, gone.

Gone into rain, into the mythology of Friday night
sex that never happened yet like this.

They lash down a pint, then another; she traces
sweat down a taxi window. *Where to, love?*

wakes her, the driver smiling at his meter,
slackening his turban where she'd like

to lay the lash of fuchsia lips, loosen his rope
of oiled hair, then lower herself to meet

the river's rise. But listen: she's whispering,
she's whispering. *To anywhere.*

Prodigal

The house anticipates you, its memory
bringing it from blown mist at the lane-end
where litter is caught on a hedge
and your father's car rages into rust.

Approach by apple trees where spiders
have webbed branches with a morning's
fine brocade of pearls; they part for you,
an avenue of veiled, expectant brides.

First sparrows hunger under dawn's
uncrumpled sheets of silk; no stirrings
from the house, though one light left on
still signals from a room of books.

An hour's wait. Quotidian things amaze:
the radio's blurred tongue, the scent of
burning toast, the swish of curtain rings,
your father's voice the same.

Your mother rises to her children's milk-
teeth smiles, shrugs into a damson
dressing gown – that Christmas gift – clearing
her hair from its collar, careless as a girl.

Here is the house: its spare-room duvet
folded back, its cupboard of broken toys,
bicycles outgrown in the garden shed, a
half-built glider hanging in the attic room.

Lives resume, grow back towards themselves
the way house-plants grope for light; now
rays delineate the lawn, dowse a gutter, gild
the door knocker where your hand tries

to rap an entrance but falls away instead.
This house with its coffee cups, its blue fume
of iris in a vase, its hush of order. The way they
rush to the phone, catching a child's voice

in the man's, anxious for everything in lives
that rushed past theirs. Go in. This is your
room, rearranging its furniture over plain rugs,
hanging old pictures on new-painted walls.

Go in to take your mother's tears, your father's
paper hand, their questions abbreviating a
journey of lost years to this moment in a place
you need to stay but can't, and cannot need.

Sweat awake at night, grope for a glass
where the fridge hums incantations of ice,
where thoughts melt to a water-stain map
of somewhere else you'd like to be.

In the morning, mist clamps the trees again,
your mother steams creases from a blouse,
your father whistles from the garden, tending
a fire of leaves which hardly yet begin to fall.

This house where nothing happens now,
freighted with forgiveness. This house of
open doors, and broken bread. This house
where you must wake and learn to breathe again.

Night Rain

We won't talk about rain at night,
its sibilant whispers at the very
dead of hearing,

nor speak of rain at dawn, its
harshness, its unforgiving nature
ushering in the light.

Today rain pearls on window-glass,
sweat's incense on a temple of
difficult thoughts.

And today we're walking again,
not mentioning the hedgerows,
their meadowsweet and berry blossom,

their herb robert, honeysuckle
and hawthorn, their rank grass
smelling of wet days.

Tomorrow we'll speak of nothing else,
list the hedgerow's scents, kiss
easy rain from each others' mouths;

we won't talk about time left,
about sea-fret, the sea lost out there,
ticking at the shoreline stones.

Pianoforte

Big in the music business, our father
once kept thirteen pianos in the house.

People found this hard to believe, so we
pictured it for them: a house never short
of ivory or ebony, our fingers waltzing over
slave-trade arpeggios; a house where we
dined from the lid of a baby Broadwood,
skated to school on the Steinway's
borrowed castors, stood pianos on pianos –
the mini-piano inside the concert grand –
and at night whispered the scary German
consonants which captured sleep.

On winter evenings we lit candles in ornate
brass brackets, softening the rooms with
Edwardian light, with homesick songs of
patriotic loss, even employed a blind piano
tuner who only worked at night, each dawn
stepping over traps of snapped strings where
he'd tempered scales to pour cornflakes
or grill toast, the daylight he couldn't see
twisting down figured walnut legs.

My parents slept or argued or made love
on a Bechstein's broken sound-board, behind
a bedroom door of lacquered panels inlaid
with *fleur de lis*; how much of our childhood
was pianissimo, the timbre of felted hammers
falling, how much spent listening then, we never
say, hearkening for wrong chords to brood,
gather, darken the piano's terrible voice.

Thorpenesse

Here at the world's edge the moon was almost full
last night, dragging its trail across the sea, pulling
stunned water into shingle's finned arêtes.

It laid a tide of flotsam at the beach: bladderwrack,
dismembered crabs, cuttlefish, driftwood, turds of
engine oil, peat-cobs, a woman's shoe cargoed by

longshore drift. Now a message in a bottle weighted
with stones. It must have bobbed gleaming in that
glare of moon as we made love so unexpectedly,

fallen into sleep until the edges of our dreams touched
to wake us. Afterwards, we rose, opened curtains,
watched a trawler lit from bow to stern riding out the

swell, its fairground gaiety stilled by salt, night's depth,
uncertain dark. The treasure map parts in your hands,
shows a skull, crossed bones, a windmill, the marsh

where whatever is buried sinks under its portentous
scarlet cross. The way things look it didn't get far, just
lilted back to the same beach; maybe those kids knew

the sleight-of-hand of tides and planned it this way,
or maybe hoped to beach their riddle someplace far off
they imagined a curious people were, eyes turned to

the cult of equinoctial seas. Curious, the way last night
I laid my ear to your breastbone to find what I've always
sought beyond fathomable skin, your deft hands

signalling unsaid things. I heard blood ebbing then rising
with each emission of your heart, that's all. Today we're
gathering sea-coal, spars of jet, amber and amethyst.

Waves furl, rub pebbles into grains of scarcely diminished
time, infinite worlds whose horizons can't hide the ancient
stare of newness in the dawn. The sea glitters, a fishing boat

drops its nets. You're signalling another find, waving from
the spray of a clouded sky towards something far out
for which words have blown over or away.

Notes on the London Underground

We float face-up in windows on the Tube,
past cables pumped-out like a junkie's arm;
no talk, just wheels on steel, the hiss of
brakes pressing with their insane calm.

Workmen in Day-Glo orange coats are here,
restoring something among ghostly crowds;
above this tunnel's held-back tons of clay
are city spires still reaching for the clouds.

Madonna of wraiths, that woman paints her lips,
a mirror pixillates to dust-motes in her palm –
event-horizon of a hole we travel in, not through.
She dabs on mascara's voodoo charm.

Brake linings burn, we stall, shunt forward,
touch, avoid each other's eyes or stare where
hoardings sell the city to itself, until Bacardi,
Coke, and Palm Beach holidays become a blur.

At Charing Cross we step through shushing
doors into a prickly, feral heat. There's nowhere
now to go but up; we file through turnstiles,
spill as surplus change onto the street.

Released, we breathe monoxide air where
sky is carbonised by dusk. The homeless
crouch in doorways, endure days designed
to strip the kernel from the husk.

Prohibition

The day the booze ran out we tore
every copy of that banning order down,
that doomed decree flyposted across this
overheated, flyblown, stinking town.

At first an aspirin clarity, as if those
were the first unclouded thoughts
we'd ever had, then the slow scald of un-
quenched thirst blistering our throats.

Inventive, we drank thermometers,
distilled demijohns of pure methanol,
made solvent cocktails that left us
prophetically blind, but didn't kill.

Sightless, we sucked neon from
billboard lights, a Las Vegas Sling
that lifted us to pyrotechnic heights,
to miracles no alcohol could bring.

Then one visionary soul earthed himself
to the town's high-tension cables and we
got high on schooners of his piss, like
Berserkers in those fly agaric fables.

We got the taste for it alright, reclined
in bathtubs with curling toes, listening
to what the stars sobbed and sang to us
through submersed, mains-wired radios.

When the ban was lifted, every bar we
stumbled to seemed muzaked, placid.
Stuff vodka – we twirled zinc cocktail
stirrers in slammers of sulphuric acid.

Which, with votive insouciance
we tossed off neat, then clasping arms
flocked like inebriate, dusk-drawn bats to
the drunken celebration of the street.

Now cancered prostates have done for
almost all our dwindling club, Homeric piss-
artists who had the guts for sable brushes
to light the deathly static at life's hub.

New generations grow: when we're spark-out
on funeral biers, our black-gloved acolytes
will volley shots of liquid oxygen to cheer us
through eternal nights.

Cuba Libre at the Café España

Catalunya

The airbus engines hush their steel-choir
drone, turbos blur to visibility, wheels
risk a kiss, get tactile, touch-down
at Perpignan: its saffron streets
and firefly cars, its runways flaring
below our wing, its southern
night exhaling light.

Then the autoroute's static
of French DJ's, its Babel
of rock-music and rising heat,
our map spread across your English knees,
the politics of the wheel between us.
Headlights unfurl rock, scrub pines,
flat-tongued cacti lolling where a border guard
waves us past stalled lorries, loosing Spanish verbs
from the bored threshold of his world.

Catalunya fills the car with sea, dust, acacia scent
and death, each moment of spiced air arriving
through rolled-down windows to wake us;
villas balanced on cliffs, hillsides quarried
from the roads, fishing boats far out
from land lamping a squid-ink sea.

The coast road spirals to the village,
its houses shuttered, its narrow streets'
nocturnal life serene with sleepers'
unpronounceable dreams.
Gossip is banished from cafés,
the church emptied of praise,
though dawn's thanksgiving
already glimmers on pantile roofs.

In ten years Castillian has vanished;
street-names lose us in risen Catalan
until the car fumbles us up a cobbled hill
to unlock the flat's terminal heat, shower,
then taste the sudden sweat of sleep.

Port de la Selva

We wake to a brutal day, the bay
stinging with light scrubbed to splinters
over fibre-glass hulled waves.

A hillside of vines chokes in ochre dust;
traffic burning the air, masts chiming,
sun incinerating sea's prophecy of calm.

The village seethes with its woken multitude,
its dead-fish stench of waste-bins sickening
our appetite for coffee, *crusantes*, bread.

Cafés are wanton with speech, sea
whispers at the quayside's confessional,
fishermen search their nets, pour
a silver night onto snow.

Streetwise

The cats here are lean, step warily;
streets tilt their cobbles at a scalded sky,
slipways for the launching sun.

Cats duck the glare of white walls,
circle outer-edges, frontiers of scent, history's
invisible palisades.

Anonymous, we brush the limits
of language's sea-worthiness or purpose,
the simple numbness of hot stone.

Cats stroll to waste-bins, finnick
the mercurial rot of sardine heads,
their stink a gauze of denser air.

Cats outstare the day's exclusion zone,
watch swifts air-blade terracotta roofs
in a blurred heat-haze of wings.

Snorkelling

Sails gavotte the sea's chipped glaze;
snorkellers paddle out, glimpsing swimmers' legs,
sea urchins, jellyfish veils,
claws that scuttle up a sediment
the sea lets slowly fall.

I'm caressing sun-cream onto your
shoulders' freckled skin,
watching two women wince over shingle
to the water's hem; the eldest mottled
the plum colour of falling fruit,
her daughter ripening an identical smile
at the sea's petulance.

Delighted by the tang of waves the old woman sinks
forward, tattooed by her own veins, sculling
in slow strokes to an horizon of tinder hills
smouldering in surf.

Last night we lay in the din
of unsleeping Spaniards dining late;
this morning I kissed your belly, water-
marked where our children swam out to nets
we couldn't guess away.

Those youngsters jack-knife from rock,
their bodies oiled, water-borne, careless,
the French girls glazed as new bread,
the Spanish boys watching them
with eyes of startled blue.

Flippers semaphore another sub-aqueous
surprise – something else ecstatically
alive beyond your skin's heat,
those women spitting water,
the sails' *paso doble*
over waves' applause.

Storm

Shutters slam under the first clenched
fist of wind, rain rinsing dust from streets
from parched roofs where gulls scream
at sheet lightning shocking
the *flambé* of the sea.

This is God showing us something beyond reason,
beyond the mere facts of updraft,
electrified ice, charged air;
static lifts your hair, thunder bursts
the mountains' brittle bubble-wrap.

Wind shakes everything the town leaves loose:
trees, shop signs, litter, the frocks of girls
speeding home on mopeds; darkness
is a sudden thumbprint inking the town
and I know whatever we're looking for is here,
suddenly close as inheld breath.

A drenched expectancy,
that fist again, then rain's dialectic pattering,
the way thoughts unsoothe a mind
used to the stillness of elsewhere.

We try to sleep, chilled in the tiled apartment;
you're cradled in some dream
like a stranger dozing on a train,
my hand on your hip, your body cool
between the cotton touch of sheets.

This morning, clouds shrink from the bay's
douche of blue, heat distilling purer air,
the monastery gaping on its spoiled mountain,
its terraces falling, its villas
shining in their duplicate glory.

Longitude

Forty-two today, the middle-age I thought
would never come or feel was really here;
strolling down a cobbled street at some point of time
or longitude, rain guttering over steps, a dead swift
washed outstretched to the sea.

All night you held my hand, tugged my thumb
like a child's mouth suckling,
one shoulder bare when dawn breezed in.
This morning I have a birthday to surprise me
with another year, my father's face peering
through the bathroom mirror's mist.

I'm smiling, amazed
at myself still alive, a stranger here,
a boy in my man's body,
walking to the shops to bring back milk,
this bread still warm under
my blue shirt blooming with rain.

Fire Festival

All night mopeds putter in the street,
a salsa band's bass-lines throb from
the beach where fire-eaters jay-walk
swigging paraffin, gobbing flame –
los diablos – lurching from shadow
to shadow, their faces painted
against the light.

The crowd's last *sardane*
leaves the town too hot to sleep,
think, make love; sheets shroud us,
sweating out the sea we swam in.

A half-moon laps at us
like a pale, aristocratic cat;
we sleep fitfully, wake fevered,
night-sweats quickening our hearts,
dawn's chill on damp pillows.

Rain varnishes the street, liquefied light
streaming over slantwise stone;
now you are calmly noticing me,
something the night left unexplained
in your bed.
Moon's counter weight raises the sun;
our mouths bitter as peach-stones,
your stung lips tender to the kiss.

Anchovies

Anchovies are sea's calcification,
their bones crushed between our teeth,
their spines salting the slugs
of our tongues.

We slice flesh,
defibrillate pink tissue;
you're describing something out there
in the world and I'm hardly listening,
watching your lips flinch,
glossed by wine.

Such a dry sting: the tang of sloes
bitten from thorns, the tongue's winding
gear rusted, speech seized
in the sea-wrecked skull.

Past cutlery shoals, lawn tablecloths, cane chairs,
past our bottle of Pescador
in its sleeve of ice
hillsides stiffen with the slow sucking
of olive trees and emerald pines.

Now a sea is withering in our heads,
its nacre polishing our mouths;

eye to eye across this café table
we swallow an ocean, a desert,
a desert, an ocean.

Wild Grapes

Scrub explodes in splinters of green;
hillsides trickle dust, a lizard coils
its false tail under a prickly pear.

Even rock is aromatic with sun;
oils of lavender and rosemary sublime
into superheated air, arthritic
roots haul us up a gully that sheds sweat
and stones under our feet.

These hillsides were terraced for vines
gone wild long since; here is what labour
comes to in the end, its forsaken love,
the scars of some lost wine war
with France.

Wild grapes are too sour for pressing;
they've strayed from the knife,
from grafting onto newer stock;
those cellars where cases of wine
and rifles were laid down
fall inwards onto darkness now.

The years that propped their vaults
– the constant temperature of air –
saw the sown stones of hope crushed, until
wishes sent after the old language returned,
bringing the *Garnacha* of speech
to christen its own elusiveness.

Air is resinous with scent,
a hawk drifts in your caught breath,
your knees gleaming as I wait for you,
watching the beach's turning
tide of flesh.

Cuba Libre at the Café España

Café España:
its dazzle of aluminium,
polished steel, the glossy insouciance
of waiters, their high voices
pitching orders to the bar.

You order *Cuba libre*
in half decent Castillian
your hand on mine as rum,
and ice jostle in a glass;
I sip a bleary beer
stare out at fishing boats
unpacking the night's catch,
each fish body nickel-bright
as change from a suddenly
remembered dream.

The light is too much;
too blinding a day, too little to say;
we unfold the map,
searching for the name of a place
the place of a name:
Figueres, Peralada, Cadaqués,
those bays infolding, those roads
winding towards each other,
like the sense of touch
through sleep.

I'm watching you announce
the day's coordinates,
your lips wet with liberty,
my finger tracing the circle
your glass just left.

La Vida Breve

Church stones humidify;
dusk is wringing out the day's
sweat to holiness.

A Barcelona wind-band plays
under windows reglazed from
republican rifle-butts.

A bloated moon lies face-up
on the bay; fishing boats
bait the sea with light.

Christ is still as a moth,
a lepidopterist's exact passion, pinned
above barbed wire thorns.

Bullets are stilled here, hate hidden,
the brindled blood of fratricide
drained to sacrament.

Here the señoras cool Falla's dance,
their fans an elegant, synchronised
farewell.

A bat flickers out above the altar,
buffeted by rapid hands, not knowing
its wings are banned here –

it should be music unites us, Christ's
pained forgiveness, but what moves our
heads in unison is a bat

rising in music's thermals – Shostakovich's
sad polka, its rhythm of shuffling
suspects chained.

A girl who lay topless on the beach
an hour ago flicks back her hair
and sighs.

Your eyes close, intent and tearful
at our last night in this place;
the bat's wings ululate a silence
an echoed ecstasy
of space.

The Sea Road

An empty bed, sun stripping
the bay, already the steady insinuation
of ascending heat.

We drag our bags to the car
wind down windows,
throttle slowly to the harbour
where we hand in keys and fishermen
smoke a last cigarette, staring at the sea
which carried away their lives.

The road is a hasty lick of tar
sticky as a toad's tongue
above the Med,
taking us hostage at every bend
and swirl.

Soon we'll be knuckling our eyes,
breakfasting on *café solo* at Portbou;
then the gendarme flipping our ID
over the border into France,
your tanned arms at the wheel,
the day so lovely with loss
we hardly talk.

Later our plane will lift us into drizzle,
over the Channel's crinkled foil,
the Saxon fields of Kent.

Another day of driving north
then Yorkshire towns and hills,
their stone capes drawn tight against rain
and too much hope.

Not yet:
a kestrel's compass needle flickers
over the bay's salvation of calm,
its plumage blistering in scorched air,
our wheels squirting stones
from the road, the sea glittering
in shattered chains of light.

Acknowledgements

Acknowledgements are due to the editors of the following publications where some of these poems first appeared: *Boomerang, Dhana, Dreamcatcher, Envoi, Pitch, Poetry News, Poetry Review, Poetry Wales, Pretext, Prop, Smiths Knoll, The Interpreter's House, The North, The Rialto.*

'Cuba Libre at the Café España' was commissioned for the Poetry Society Poetry Places website at:
www.poetrysociety.org.uk/places/placeind.htm

Poems from the sequence formed part of the BBC Radio 4 play of the same name, broadcast in April 2002. The sequence was also shortlisted in the *Blue Nose Poets* Competition, 2000.

'Washdays' was shortlisted in the *Stand* International Poetry Competition, 2000.

Many thanks to the Aldeburgh Poetry Trust for the Aldeburgh Poetry Festival Residency, 2000, which allowed me time to work on this collection.